Original title:
Dandelion Daydreams

Copyright © 2025 Creative Arts Management OÜ
All rights reserved.

Author: Nolan Kingsley
ISBN HARDBACK: 978-1-80567-000-1
ISBN PAPERBACK: 978-1-80567-080-3

Over the Horizon of Iridescent Skies

Balloons float high, a curious sight,
Chasing the clouds, they take flight.
A squirrel dons a tiny hat,
What next? A dog? Perhaps a cat!

Sunlight giggles, the breeze pretends,
As shadows dance, the laughter bends.
Joy hops along on rainbow beams,
In this playful world of silly dreams.

Chasing Fables in the Wild

A rabbit wears spectacles, reads a tale,
While frogs in tuxedos set off to sail.
They giggle and croak with fancy flair,
In their own whimsical, joyous air.

The trees whisper secrets, branches clap,
As gnomes gather round for a nap and a snack.
With twinkling eyes and mischief afloat,
They plan a feast on a huge, leafy boat.

The Ethereal Artistry of Nature

Butterflies paint with colors so bold,
While bees hum tunes of stories untold.
A snail wearing boots struts down the lane,
Singing a tune that tickles the brain.

The flowers giggle in bright purple hats,
As daisies joke with the friendly hyenas.
They dance in the breeze, a cacophony sweet,
Creating a ruckus beneath tiny feet.

Sunlight and Shadows Together

Sunshine naps on the soft, green grass,
While shadows tell jokes that make time pass.
A ladybug juggles with tiny glee,
As ants plan a circus for all to see.

The day wears a grin, the stars peek through,
A comet winks, 'I'll join the fun too!'
Nature chuckles, 'What a time to play!'
In this realm of giggles, come join the fray!

Swaying Dreams Under the Blue

In a field where wishes play,
Tiny seeds drift on ballet,
Tickled by the summer breeze,
Searching hearts for laughs and ease.

With every puff, the giggles rise,
Squinting up at sunny skies,
They twirl and swirl, a jolly game,
Each one whispers a silly name.

Butterflies join the silly dance,
Floating lightly, taking a chance,
While ants wear hats, and grasshoppers sing,
Life's just better when you're in spring.

So let those puffs take flight and roam,
For in their journey, find your home,
A silly leap, a joy unfurled,
Swaying dreams in a playful world.

The Art of Letting Go

Release your worries, let them fly,
Like fluffy clouds in a clear blue sky,
Each seed a thought, light as a string,
Floating far, come back next spring.

We cling to dreams like kids to swings,
But humor blooms from all these things,
Watch them dance and twirl away,
Laughing at the games they play.

A gust of wind, a tickling breeze,
Whispers jokes that put you at ease,
Let go your troubles, wave them bye,
Join the fun in a carefree sigh.

So take a breath, surrender tight,
In laughter's grasp, find pure delight,
As every wish finds place to grow,
The art of life is the art of flow.

Infinite Whispers of Tomorrow

Each whisper spins a tale so bright,
Tickling ears with pure delight,
Floating notions, crazy schemes,
Crafting laughter from wild dreams.

Tomorrow's whispers bring surprise,
A tickle in the morning rise,
Seedlings dance to stories told,
In playful jest, their joy unfolds.

With every breeze, a cunning twist,
Thoughts like bubbles, can't resist,
A hop, skip, jump, they come alive,
In the wild chaos, spirits thrive.

So let the whispers pull you near,
Where laughter sings, and joy is clear,
In infinite tales each moment glows,
With secrets carried wherever it goes.

Soft Echoes of Childhood's Laughter

In the meadow, giggles soar,
Childhood echoes, tales galore,
A sprinkle of joy in every dance,
As we twirl in a silly trance.

Spinning dreams beneath the trees,
Chasing shadows, feeling the breeze,
Time sprints by, but we hold fast,
To that sweet laughter, pure and vast.

With every pop and every puff,
Life's a game, never too tough,
Two-step whimsies, we declare,
Fun is found in everywhere.

So gather round, let laughter flow,
In the echo of a child's glow,
As soft whispers blend in the air,
Never forget the joy we share.

Curiosities of the Gentle Wind

A puff of air, what will it do?
It tickles my nose, then sneezes too.
Whirling around, a goofy twist,
What secret paths have I missed?

Whispers of laughter, trees bend low,
Chasing their shadows, away they go.
A tumbleweed's dance, a skip, a sway,
Is it the wind, or just me at play?

Look, a paper plane, wild and free,
Took off with glee, where could it be?
The breeze is a joker, with tricks to share,
It winks and whispers, "You've got flair!"

Frolicking leaves, oh what a sight,
They twirl and spin from morning till night.
In this merry chase, who shall prevail?
The wind or me, on this silly trail?

Sunswept Sagas Beneath the Sky

Under the sun, the laughter erupts,
Silly asterisks, in soft flower cups.
Bumblebees buzzing, they wear tiny hats,
Playing card games with the nearby cats.

Butterflies boast in their colorful suits,
Dancing on petals, gossiping roots.
With each little flit, a story is spun,
Sharing tall tales of a flower's run.

A sunbeam hops, like a child in play,
Chasing the clouds, making them sway.
Giggles erupt as shadows stretch long,
In this kaleidoscope, we all belong.

Oh what a jest, beneath skies so clear,
Every giggle and dance brings us near.
With laughter our guide, come join the fun,
For every bright day is a quest begun!

Meadow's Lullaby of Imagination

In fields of gold, the tickles ensue,
Popping up dreams like bubbles, woohoo!
A rabbit hops high, with goggle-eyed flair,
Wondering why humans just sit and stare.

The flowers are chatting, oh what a group,
Creating a ruckus, forming a hoop.
They giggle and jostle, petals in tow,
While ants do a march, in perfect row.

Clouds drift above, wearing hats made of cream,
Winking at daisies in the sunlight beam.
A parade of ideas, so colorful and bright,
Imagination reigns in the soft golden light.

So lay in the grass, let your thoughts take flight,
Join the meadow's tale, it's pure delight.
For in this kingdom of whimsy and cheer,
Every little giggle brings the world near!

Dreams of a Sun-Kissed Meadow

In a meadow bright, where the clovers play,
Bumblebees dance, buzzing their ballet.
Tiny bugs gather for a picnic feast,
While grasshoppers cheer, saying, "Grab a seat!"

Laughter bursts out from a butterfly's crown,
Wings painted with joy, fluttering around.
The daisies giggle, tickling the breeze,
As sunbeams join in, whirling with ease.

Floating Seeds of Hope

A whisper of wishes on the warm, soft air,
Seeds tumble and twirl, without a care.
They plot their own journeys, oh, what a thrill,
"Let's float to the moon!" they say with goodwill.

Splattered with laughter, they dance on the wind,
Wondering where their wild travels will end.
Across fields and gardens, the dreams come alive,
"Catch me if you can!" the tiny hopes strive.

Wishes in the Wildflower Fields

In fields of wildflowers, wishes are sewn,
With petals and giggles, together they've grown.
A snail joins the party, wearing a shell,
While ladybugs gossip, oh, do tell, do tell!

The sun's a big joker, peeking through the trees,
Tickling the blooms in a warm, gentle tease.
Frolicsome critters join in for a chase,
As butterflies blurt out, "Let's pick up the pace!"

Echoes of Springtime Promises

The echoes of laughter fill the bright air,
Spring's playful promises, floating everywhere.
A squirrel dons shades, striking a pose,
While frogs hold a concert, in tiny, wet clothes.

Crickets compose tunes, oh what a sound!
As flowers take turns, twirling around.
With the wind as their partner, they sway and spin,
Creating a show, where giggles begin.

The Art of Letting Go

With each gust, a wish takes flight,
A tiny seed, a bold delight.
Aiming high, yet oh so low,
It's quite the art, this letting go.

The breeze giggles, carries woes,
To far-off lands where laughter flows.
In playful spins, the whims befriend,
As giggles swirl and never end.

The ground below starts to cheer,
For floating dreams bring joy near.
What once was here, now dances away,
In silly flights of carefree play.

With winks and grins, the blossoms tease,
While jumbled thoughts swirl in the breeze.
They tumble forth, no rhyme nor reason,
A whimsied mess each goofy season.

Swaying in Soft Sunshine

Beneath the sky, a golden glow,
The flowers sway, a merry show.
They twist and twirl, so light and spry,
As giggles chase the clouds on high.

The sunbeams laugh, they reach and tickle,
As petals dance, a joyful fickle.
Each sway a jig, a funny twist,
No flower dares to be dismissed.

With laughter caught in every bloom,
They shake their heads, dispelling gloom.
A carnival of colors bright,
In playful spins, they hug the light.

Oh, sunny day, you charm us so,
Your warmth brings forth our playful glow.
In blooming antics, life is spry,
With every twirl, we reach the sky.

Puffs of Imagination

In gentle puffs, ideas sprout,
Like little clouds of joy, no doubt.
Whispered thoughts take wing and float,
With every breeze, a silly quote.

A squiggly thought can spin awry,
As laughter dances in the sky.
With playful plumes that brush the chin,
They twirl around, let the fun begin!

What if a star could ride a kite?
Or frogs wore hats all day and night?
These whims are dreams that blow and play,
In fluffy bursts, they find their way.

Each fleeting thought, a giggle shared,
For every puff, the heart is bared.
In flights of fancy, we dare to see,
The silly worlds that could just be.

In the Heart of a Whispering Field

In fields where whispers softly sway,
The flowers gossip all the day.
They share the news, the sweetest joke,
With every petal, laughter's stoke.

A tumbleweed comes rolling by,
It trips and spins, oh my, oh my!
With raucous laughs, it brings a cheer,
The field erupts; the fun is near.

A ticklish breeze runs through the air,
And all the blooms begin to share.
With bright-eyed mirth, they nod their heads,
As every whim makes silly threads.

Together here, under the sun,
With all their quips, they're just such fun.
In whispered tales of joy and grace,
They watch the clouds in a playful race.

A Voyage on Petal Wings

On a whim, we sail so high,
With petals catching dreams that fly.
We laugh as we dip and dive,
In silly flights, we come alive.

Breeze tickles our toes, what a treat!
We're monarchs of the grassy seat.
Chasing clouds, making them giggle,
Where every twist makes our hearts wiggle.

Sunshine winks from overhead,
Waving like it's in a thread.
In this vessel made of light,
We'll drift through the day and into the night.

With feathered friends, we share our song,
Swaying to rhythms, bright and strong.
Each moment twists with silly glee,
In our petal boat sailing free!

Beneath a Blanket of Cloud Cotton

Lying low on a fluffy shore,
We bounce with the clouds, wanting more.
Each puffy tuft a silly friend,
In our cotton world, we'll pretend.

We poke a pie in a cloud's face,
And giggle as we join the race.
Floating high, then falling down,
We're kings and queens of fluff-town crown!

Sunbeams dance through our soft cover,
Painting shadows of lovers who hover.
We tickle the sky and twist just right,
Making the day bloom with delight.

Time plays tricks with sticky feet,
Chasing the breeze, a tasty treat.
With every jump and every twirl,
Under our blanket, we laugh and whirl!

Enchanted Moments in the Meadow

In the meadow where giggles grow,
We prance where the wild daisies blow.
The grass plays tunes beneath our toes,
As we dance where the soft wind blows.

Bouncing over blades like silly frogs,
Waving at passing, curious dogs.
Every bud whispers a cheeky secret,
In giggles, we find the perfect pocket!

Here sunshine pours like honey streams,
We sip on laughter and sweet daydreams.
And with every whimsical swirl,
We twist like ribbons—oh, let's twirl!

"More bubbles," we shout, with voices bright,
Chasing the butterflies, pure delight.
In this meadow of joys to pluck,
Every moment's a little bit of luck!

Meadow's Elfin Secrets

Whispers flutter like the leaves,
In the meadow where mischief weaves.
Here elves play tricks, behind each tree,
With twinkling eyes, they beckon me.

A hopscotch made of sunbeam dreams,
With giggling shadows and laughing streams.
We trip on laughter, fall in cheer,
Every riddle brings us near!

They slip through flowers, quick as light,
With jests that tickle hearts outright.
As they crown our heads with clover crowns,
We dance like silly little clowns.

In this haven of leafy glee,
The elves are friends and wild and free.
With every wink, the world feels bright,
Secrets shared in the soft moonlight!

A Dance Amongst the Starlit Clusters

In a field where whispers play,
Tiny wishes drift away.
Stars twinkle like painted hues,
While giggles ride the evening's muse.

Moonlight wraps the world in glee,
As night's parade begins to spree.
With every puff, a tale is spun,
Of humor found in twilight fun.

Bouncing dreams like popcorn balls,
They leap and twirl, they spin and fall.
Caught in laughter, a joyous race,
Each tiny puff, a smiling face.

As shadows dance in silly shapes,
The air is filled with funny drapes.
In this nonsense, joy's revealed,
A nightly frolic, magic field.

Floating Fantasies in the Springtime

With laughter woven through the air,
Some dreams choose to tag and share.
Puffy parachutes of zest,
Tumble forth to blissful rest.

Sprouting joy on every breeze,
Frolicking through the trees with ease.
They chase the sun, a wild flight,
Tickling petals, pure delight.

Colors burst with silly sounds,
As nature's whimsy knows no bounds.
Whispers echo with each prance,
In spring's embrace, all dreams dance.

A floating smile on every seed,
Painting the sky with hope's good need.
So come and join this jest-filled day,
Where laughter leads and worries sway.

Fluttering Hopes in Nature's Arms

In grassy realms where creatures tease,
Silly breezes play with ease.
Wobbly wishes in the air,
Bouncing gently, floating fair.

A tickle here, a giggle there,
Sprinkled joy beyond compare.
As fluffy dreams take flight and sway,
The world is bright in capers' play.

Every gust a cheerful song,
As dance partners leap along.
In Nature's arms, we find the cheer,
With every smile, the laughter's clear.

So chase the hopes through fields so wide,
With jigs and japes that can't abide.
Join the frolic, take your stand,
In dreams so playful, hand in hand.

The Playfulness of Wayward Seeds

Wayward seeds with playful flair,
Tumble down without a care.
Each one seeks a friend to play,
In sunny fields, they sway away.

Joking with the light and air,
Silly twirls without a scare.
With every puff, a wink they send,
So joyful, mischief is their trend.

Bouncing high on giggles bright,
They swirl and dance in sheer delight.
A playful race through blades of green,
In every flight, a silly scene.

So join the jest of buttercups,
As laughter spills from morning cups.
With every leap and thrilling chase,
Embrace the joy, let worries erase.

Moments Spun from Gold

In fields of fluff where giggles soar,
A bumblebee begs for just one more.
He lands on a flower, takes a spin,
Then trips on a petal; oh, let the fun begin!

A child with a wish, eyes round as a plate,
Blows out her dreams; will they float or just wait?
The wind plays a trick, they scatter and swerve,
And land on a dog that decides to observe!

Laughter erupts at this curious sight,
As the dog chases wishes into the night.
Every puff carries stories untold,
Moments like these are shiny as gold!

So let us rejoice in this playful parade,
For life is a whimsy, and joy is its grade.
In the dance of the seeds, delight takes a hold,
As each little wish becomes a tale to unfold.

Ephemeral Escapes

Tiny anchors drift on the breeze,
Tickling noses of children with ease.
A burst of laughter, a caper or two,
And soon they decide to join in the view.

Shades of yellow, a blanket of cheer,
Kids dive through fluff, their giggles sincere.
Chasing the puffs with eyes full of glee,
They waltz with the wind, oh what a spree!

A puppy joins in with a comical bark,
Bounding through air like a shot in the dark.
Fluffy balls dance, then tumble to land,
In this peculiar, jubilant band!

Oh fleeting delights, like popcorn in flight,
They vanish too soon, yet feel oh so right.
Let's capture this moment, no time to escape,
With laughter and joy; let's seal up the tape!

The Dance of the Wandering Seeds

Little seeds twirl on a stage of the sky,
With pirouettes bold, they flutter and fly.
A dance of the tiny, a whirlwind of fun,
Their giggles a chorus beneath the warm sun.

A gust sweeps through, with a tickle and tease,
And off they all go like a playful sneeze.
Chasing each other through trees and the grass,
Who knew such small things could have such pizzazz?

Watch closely, dear friend, as they put on a show,
With each little tumble, their joy starts to grow.
They'll land where they may, in a child's wild play,
Creating more laughter than clouds on a day!

So revel in moments of whimsy and cheer,
For these little dancers will soon disappear.
But don't you fret not, in your heart they will stay,
A reminder to play, come what may!

Beneath the Sky's Embrace

Fluffy parachutes sway in the air,
Underneath giggles, let's dance without care.
With every soft puff, a wish takes its flight,
Floating like dreams in the warm sunlit light.

A squirrel in a hat, with a glint in his eye,
Joins in the fun, as he leaps oh so spry.
He twirls with the seeds, then trips on a leaf,
And rolls in the grass, a true comic relief!

Children chase after, with arms open wide,
To catch them all tightly, a whimsical ride.
But the wind has a plan, a giggle in tow,
As it lifts them away, with a swift, joyful 'whoa!'

So here's to the laughter that breezes around,
To each fleeting moment in giggles profound.
Let's cherish the fun beneath sky's bright embrace,
Where whimsy and joy find their wonderful place!

Papery Fantasies of an Open Sky

A breeze rides high on cotton clouds,
Whispering secrets, giggles abound.
Petals that float like tiny boats,
Chasing sunbeams, oh how it gloats!

Laughter dances on tips of grass,
As wishes tumble, and moments pass.
Silly thoughts spin like a wheel,
In this land where joy is real.

Clouds wearing hats of marshmallow fluff,
Creating creatures, goofy and tough.
Rabbits that flip, and turtles that glide,
In this playtime, there's no need to hide.

We laugh at shadows that stretch and bend,
Sharing jests with the twilight's friend.
In this world, the absurd reigns true,
Where paper dreams are made for me and you.

Wandering Through Fields of Reverie

In a meadow where giggles bloom,
Thoughts drift freely with sweet perfume.
Bouncing bunnies in a silly race,
Chasing giggles, a wild embrace.

Clouds tease the sun, play hide and seek,
While butterflies giggle, tiny and meek.
A wind that tickles, a dance of cheer,
Through fields of whimsy, we have no fear.

Straw hats lounge on the laughing grass,
Collecting thoughts as the moments pass.
Dreams painted bright in playful hues,
Every glance tells a tale, brand new.

With each step, the world seems to say,
Life's a joke, come join the play!
In this maze of memory, we twirl,
As laughter unfurls, we spin and whirl.

Hues of the Enchanted Afternoon

Colors explode, a palette so rich,
Sunshine and giggles, a magical pitch.
Fluffy clouds wear shades of delight,
Twirling whispers that dance in the light.

Bumbles buzz like the silliest song,
As breezes hum the tunes all day long.
In each corner, quirkiness reigns,
Tickling toes and playful refrains.

A parade of daisies, topsy-turvy sprout,
Where silly hats giggle and shout.
Ribbons that swirl in a carefree spin,
An afternoon dance where all can win.

With laughter like bubbles that burst in the sky,
We bounce on dreams as they drift by.
In this vibrant realm, let worries stray,
As the hues intoxicate, come join the play.

The Path of Sweet Remembrance

On a winding trail of ticklish grass,
Memories bubble, as moments pass.
Footprints left from laughter cases,
Chasing shadows with silly faces.

A picnic spread in the shade of cheer,
With cupcakes that giggle and ice cream dear.
Jellybean roads where candy grows wild,
Echo the laughter of every child.

Every flower tells a story true,
Of heartfelt moments shared by two.
As bare feet dance on soft, green beds,
We steal a kiss, and laughter spreads.

With pockets full of whimsical dreams,
And paper boats sailing on moonlit streams,
We wander the path where memories play,
In fields of forever, let's skip away.

Memory's Sway in a Flourished Field

In a field of bright and sunny cheer,
A seed took flight, oh so near!
It danced on air with little care,
Tickling noses, hearts laid bare.

Of whimsical hops and leaps so spry,
A gust of wind made it fly high,
It twirled around, a tiny joke,
Leaving giggles in every poke.

To catch it was a funny chase,
With hands outstretched, a silly race,
But laughter filled the air instead,
As it floated off, light as a thread.

Each twist and turn, such wild delight,
In nature's joy, we take our flight,
With memory's sway, we find our way,
Through fields of fun, come what may.

Laughter in the Garden of Dreams

In a garden with whims in bloom,
A joke sprouted, dispelling gloom,
The petals cracked a playful grin,
As giggles traveled on the wind.

Butterflies wore funny hats,
While worms pretended to be cats,
A creeping vine told tales so grand,
Of adventures in a far-off land.

Every flower wore a silly face,
Enticing bees to join the race,
With buzzing laughs, they danced around,
In this garden, joy abounds.

So come and play where whimsy reigns,
In laughter's reach, forget your pains,
In this realm where fun's the theme,
We'll laugh together, chase the dream.

Whims of the Wandering Breezes

The breezes blow with cheeky cheer,
Tugging at hats, causing a sneer,
With a flip, it sways tall grass,
A playful wink as it doth pass.

Whispers of laughter fill the air,
As squirrels dance without a care,
They chase the wind, a jolly spree,
To catch the breeze, oh what a feat!

Blown leaves tickle the earth below,
In this merry, swirling show,
Each gust a giggle, a vibrant tease,
In nature's chorus, hear the breeze.

So let us whirl, in shadows play,
With joy and laughter leading the way,
For every sway and every song,
In wandering whims, we all belong.

Petals Unseen by the Naked Eye

Tiny dreams hide in the green,
With a twinkle, they're rarely seen,
A world of giggles in each bud,
Waiting for a gentle thud.

"Oh look!" cried a kid with glee,
"A petal danced, it beckons me!"
But only shadows filled the space,
Their laughter echoed, quickening pace.

In this land of jest and whim,
Invisible blooms dance on a limb,
With silken whispers in the air,
Playing tricks, oh do beware!

In playful wonder, hearts abide,
With each petal, a joy-filled ride,
For what seems lost to weary sight,
Is all around in sheer delight.

Threads of Light in Cosmic Fields

In the garden of stars, a giggle flies,
Where twinkling wishes wear silly ties.
A comet plays hopscotch, skipping through space,
While aliens dance with a comical grace.

With spoons made of stardust, they serve up a feast,
Of laughter and sprinkles, a cosmic yeast.
A nebula wraps them in cotton candy,
As cosmic popcorn pops ever so handy.

When meteors tumble like clumsy old cows,
And planetoids wobble with interstellar vows.
The sun winks at moons, all dressed in delight,
In fields where the lightballoons float out of sight.

So come chase the shadows, let your giggles soar,
Across cosmic fields where we'll laugh and explore.
With threads of bright laughter, we'll stitch through the night,
In the universe's grasp, everything feels just right.

Sunlit Fantasies Unfurled

In sunshine-soaked meadows, we bounce like a ball,
    Chasing the giggles that rise and that fall.
With daisies in crowns, we strut through the fun,
    Creating a ruckus beneath the warm sun.

A butterfly giggles while sipping sweet juice,
    As ants throw a party, their tiny recluse.
With cakes made of nectar and funfetti dreams,
    They toast to the chuckles that nonsense redeems.

The shadows play tricks in the flickering light,
    As nothing makes sense, and everything's bright.
With sunflowers grinning and waving their leaves,
    In a world of wonders, we weave and believe.

So let's paint the skies with our laughter and cheer,
    In sunlit illusions, there's nothing to fear.
Embrace every whim that the day may bestow,
    In fantastic adventures where humor will flow.

The Bristle of Untamed Thoughts

In a whimsical forest where giggles reside,
The trees wear pink hats, all stacked up with pride.
A squirrel spins tales, a connoisseur bard,
While mushrooms play poker, their bets are quite hard.

With snickers and snorts, a bear opens his den,
Producing a ukulele for friends in a trend.
The fox brings confetti, and rabbits parade,
As a jester stands tall, with mischief displayed.

They dance on the bristles of wild, crazy thought,
As fireflies giggle, caught up in the plot.
A raccoon in spectacles, wise with a grin,
Says nonsense is just where the fun should begin.

So let's stir the mayhem with laughter and flair,
In this quirky forest with joy to share.
The world spins in circles, let's flip and let fly,
On the bristles of whimsy, together we'll try.

Windborne Echoes of Enchantment

On breezy horizons where whispers take wing,
The clouds wear mustaches, and jump as they sing.
With giggling zephyrs that tickle our toes,
Each breeze sends a chuckle, wherever it blows.

A kite shaped like pudding swoops down for a chat,
While squirrels in shades debate who's fatter than fat.
With acorns as maracas, they dance and they jive,
Echoes of laughter, the sweet scent of alive.

In a world spun of mirth, where colors collide,
Rainbows mix punchlines that no one can hide.
With whimsical echoes that brighten the day,
The wind carries laughter, come join in the play.

So let's leap through the skies, where the echoes run free,

In a realm where enchantment feels just like a spree.
With giggles and joy, we'll twirl and we'll whirl,
In the dance of the breezes, let our laughter unfurl.

Petals of a Gentle Reverie

A tumbleweed, a drift of fluff,
Goldilocks got lost, oh what a stuff!
With hats that fly and shoes askew,
We dance with whimsies, just me and you.

Chasing clouds with gleeful glee,
A kingdom built on whimsy free.
Cats wear shoes and squirrels sing,
In this delightful, crazy fling.

Down the hill, oh what a sight,
A penguin slides, just out of sight!
We'll laugh until the day is done,
With cheeky grins, it's all in fun!

Join the parade of the absurd,
Where every thought is just a word.
On a balloon, let's ride away,
And greet the silliness of day.

Floating Thoughts in the Meadow

In the meadow, thoughts take flight,
With butterflies that laugh in delight.
A rooster struts in fancy bow,
While worms recite Shakespeare, wow!

A rabbit juggles carrots with flair,
As flowers gossip without a care.
Rainbows drip from trees so tall,
While ladybugs run the carnival.

Bees buzz tunes of silly songs,
Where everyone just hums along.
The sky's a canvas, bright with dreams,
And nothing's ever what it seems.

So come and dance, just take a chance,
In this topsy-turvy, twirl and prance!
For laughter sparkles in the sun,
And in this field, we all are one.

Dreams Adrift on a Summer's Gale

In the breeze, our thoughts take sail,
On sandwiches that jiggle and wail.
Bananas in pajamas dance with grace,
While jellybeans play tag in the space.

Up in the trees, a parrot quips,
About the state of flying fish.
A turtle races, snickers abound,
As squirrels play checkers on the ground.

Our dreams are like balloons at play,
Inflated by whimsy's bright bouquet.
In this world of giggles and glee,
Nothing's quite as it seems to be.

So let's swirl on the gusty breeze,
And toast to what brings us to our knees.
With every laugh, we leave behind,
The dullest cares we ever find.

Sun-kissed Wishes Take Wing

Bouncing wishes in the sun,
With giggles that have just begun.
A pancake flips, oh what a trick,
While ants parade with a sidekick.

The sun's a smile that spreads so wide,
While pineapples wear roller skates with pride.
In this world of chaotic cheer,
Every heart can skip a beat here!

Pigs in tutus take the floor,
As laughter bursts, the skies adore.
The clouds perform a fluffy dance,
While shadows manage every prance.

Just join the fun, don't hesitate,
In this land where giggles wait!
With every wish, let's take our fling,
And fly on joy's enchanting wing.

Whispers of the Wind

In the park, a puffball flies,
It tickles noses, oh what a surprise!
Children giggle, dogs chase around,
While elders sigh at the fluff on the ground.

A tiny fairy rides on a blimp,
Sipping nectar, she starts to shrimp.
Oh, what a scene, so clumsy and bright,
As they all dance in the soft golden light.

The wind plays tricks, a cartwheel of glee,
Fluff on a jet ski, just wait and see!
Each breath is laughter, each sigh is a joke,
Who knew nature was such a dope?

The clouds join in with a playful parade,
Hats made of fluff, in sunlight they wade.
The breeze just chuckles, it's all in good fun,
As we share in this dance 'til the day is done.

Golden Wishes on the Breeze

Puffs of hope in the afternoon light,
Each little wish takes off in flight.
Sprinkled magic on the laughing grass,
Where giggling sprites tumble and pass.

A squirrel with dreams of becoming a king,
Tries to gather wishes, each soft little thing.
But the moment he leaps, away they all float,
He's left chasing dreams as he waves his coat.

A stork with style in a top hat so fine,
Whisked away by a wish, that's divine!
The trees all murmur, "What's that he's got?"
Just a wishful giggle in a fanciful spot.

As the sun dips low and the day starts to bead,
The wishes take flight, unfurling indeed.
With a wink and a nod, they're off with the breeze,
Tickling fate with such playful expertise.

Seeds of Serenity

Amidst the chaos, a seed floats by,
Wearing a cap and a cheeky sigh.
"Catch me if you can!" it sings with delight,
"I'm off to the fair, gonna dance through the night!"

A sprout on a quest, it twirls in the air,
Spinning round in a whimsical dare.
With a laugh, it races a bumblebee,
Who tries to steal glances, so utterly free.

On the garden stage, the show begins,
Seeds do the tango while the sun grins.
In the dirt, they bond, sharing dreams of the stars,
A raucous good time, no need for guitars.

As twilight descends and shadows play chess,
The seeds all gather for one final mess.
A leap into fate, a raucous good cheer,
Goodbye to the day, let the night draw near.

Flight of the Sunlit Fluff

In a field so bright, a puffball takes wing,
Spreading cheer like it's the latest thing.
It dances on air, with a giggle and twist,
Every bounce, a reminder — can you resist?

Whiffs of mischief in the light of the sun,
Spinning and twirling, it's all just for fun.
A bee with a top hat buzzes in style,
Join the parade, it beckons with a smile.

The wind plays tag, a game of escape,
Fluff in the grasses, the mischievous shape.
With the chirps and the giggles, the world feels alive,
In the great fluffy dance, that's where dreams thrive.

As twilight falls, fluff paints the sky,
Glowing like wishes, as it floats by.
With a wink and a nod, it whispers farewell,
In the heart of the night, where stories will swell.

Tapestry of Fluttering Thoughts

In fields of gold, they sway and spin,
A laugh escapes, where dreams begin.
With tiny caps, they dance in air,
Whispering secrets without a care.

A toddler chases, feigning grace,
Tripping on roots, a silly face.
The wind picks up, they scatter wide,
A bouquet of giggles, soaring beside.

The sun winks down upon the scene,
As thoughts take flight, like kites so keen.
Each fragile puff, a joke in bloom,
Filling the sky, making room.

And as they frolic on their quest,
We smile, for life's a jesting jest.
With every whiff of fluffy cheer,
We hold our wishes, ever near.

The Glee of Forgotten Wishes

A wish once whispered in a hurry,
Now floats along, a gentle flurry.
It tickles arms, and makes you grin,
Lost thoughts return, let laughter begin!

Forgotten dreams in cotton suits,
Gallivant around in springtime boots.
They caper and tumble all about,
In joyous spirals, they twist and shout.

A child points out a wish gone wild,
How nature's tricks can charm a child.
With every puff, there's magic spread,
Tickling hearts, and a smile instead.

So here's to dreams that bounce and giggle,
In fields of laughter, they twist and wiggle.
Old wishes dance, they're never done,
In the merry glow of the midday sun.

Murmurs in the Warm Embrace of Spring

In morning's glow, they sway and charm,
Casting a spell, with gentle warmth.
They sprinkle smiles like confetti bright,
With whispers of joy, they take their flight.

A puppy jumps, thinking it's a game,
Chasing fluff, oh what a shame!
They flutter past, teasing and free,
While giggles echo beneath the tree.

Each little puff, a riddle we keep,
In sun-soaked moments, rich and deep.
Breezy haikus drift through the air,
Making the day feel light as a hair.

So take a moment, let laughter sprout,
In the bloom of dreams, there's no doubt.
With every tickle, a story takes flight,
In the embrace of spring's pure delight.

Where Wishes and Wonders Merge

A whimsical gust plays hide and seek,
With wand'ring wishes and giggles weak.
They spin and twirl, like tiny sprites,
Swirling 'round in the soft daylight.

They flurry about, in trouble we find,
Sneaking a smile, oh so unrefined.
With tickled toes, they dance with flair,
In the grand escapade of open air.

Old dreams collide in a comical clash,
Chasing each other, they tumble in a flash.
A skipping spree with no one to bind,
Unruly wishes, so playful, unlined.

Among the flowers, we chuckle and sway,
In the magic of moments, come what may.
Where wonder thrives and laughter blends,
In the heart of joy, where fun never ends.

A Symphony of Sunlit Whispers

In the park where the sunbeams dance,
A squirrel with style takes a chance.
He leaps with grace, on a branch he spins,
A nut in his paws, he surely wins.

A grasshopper hums a jaunty tune,
While butterflies twirl 'neath the full moon.
The daisies giggle in the mild breeze,
As ants in a line march with expert ease.

A bumblebee joins, buzzing with flair,
Stealing nectar from flowers with care.
But his dance gets tangled, oh what a sight!
He crashes right into a joke-shop kite.

The sun dips low, casting shadows bright,
As creatures prepare to end this delight.
With laughter and whispers, the day draws tight,
In this symphony of joy, pure and light.

Timeless Tales of the Meadow

Upon a hill, where the daisies tell,
Of cowards who ran from a snail's slow shell.
A turtle, wise, with a grin so sly,
Teaches lessons with a wink of an eye.

The frogs in the pond have quite the debate,
Is it better to sing or to hop, contemplate?
They croak out opinions, some funny, some not,
While the fish just swim by, quite lost in the plot.

A pig in a top hat takes center stage,
Declaring the rules—there's nothing to gauge!
With a trot and a snort, he steals the whole show,
As the cows roll their eyes, "Oh, there he goes!"

The stars wink above, as night starts to creep,
Each creature shares tales before drifting to sleep.
With laughter and whimsy, they fondly recall,
These timeless tales that enchant one and all.

Dreams Nestled Among the Grass

In a thicket of green, a rabbit dives deep,
Chasing after dreams, without need for sleep.
He hops to the rhythm of the soft, warm earth,
It's a bouncy, curly adventure, full of mirth.

A ladybug joins, her spots bright as day,
Spinning wild stories of love and cliché.
With each tiny giggle, she flits and she flies,
Whispering secrets that twinkle like skies.

The flowers in bloom wear their best sunny hats,
While crickets perform in their shoes made of mats.
They serenade fireflies, who blink with delight,
In a waltz of the wonders that dance through the night.

In dreams of the grass, every sigh brings a cheer,
Where laughter blooms loud, banishing fear.
Imagination runs wild with whimsy and cheer,
In this world of delight, all our dreams can appear.

Where the Wishes Go to Play

In a meadow so wide, the wishes float free,
Like balloons on a string, they dance with glee.
Whispers of hope in the soft, gentle air,
All gather together, a whimsical fair.

A duck in a bowtie quacks out a tune,
While the sun grins down, bright as a cartoon.
The flowers sway gently, tapping their toes,
As the wishes spin round in graceful shows.

A caterpillar dreams of a butterfly's flight,
While slips of paper drift into the night.
Catching the stars, they twist and they twirl,
In a funny parade, oh what a whirl!

And when the day ends, the wishes all sigh,
As the moonbeam whispers, a soft lullaby.
In this playful place, where hopes glide and sway,
Tomorrow they'll dance, where wishes go play.

Celestial Fancies at Twilight

Stars giggle in the night sky,
Whispering tales as they fly.
The moon wears a cheeky grin,
While shadows hop and spin.

Crickets play a jazzy tune,
As fireflies dance beneath the moon.
A comet winks with glee,
And stardust spills like lemonade tea.

Clouds wear funny hats so bright,
Puffing like marshmallows in flight.
Dreams ride on the breeze, oh so light,
While giggles echo into the night.

In this realm of whimsy and cheer,
Nothing's serious, have no fear.
So let your laughter take the lead,
In a world where joy is guaranteed!

Fragile Flight of Forgotten Wishes

Tiny wishes drift on air,
Tickling noses without a care.
Like butterflies at a picnic feast,\nThey flutter 'round, a playful beast.

Once forgotten, now they soar,
Chasing giggles, wanting more.
They swirl in circles, spin about,
And tickle toes, oh what a rout!

A wish once lost now leads the way,
To frolic through a sunny day.
They giggle as they reach for shoes,
And dance along with sprightly views.

So catch them quick before they're gone,
These fleeting fancies that laugh and yawn.
For in a laugh, a wish is born,
With every sigh, a giggle is worn.

A Tapestry of Golden Wishes

Golden wishes weave and twine,
In a quilt of laughter, so divine.
A tapestry of dreams in bloom,
Fills the air with sweet perfume.

Paper planes made of hopes and schemes,
Soar like clouds in playful dreams.
They giggle as they twist and roll,
Painting joy in every soul.

Each wish a thread in the sun's embrace,
Spinning stories in endless space.
With colors bright and laughter loud,
Happiness weaves a glossy shroud.

So toss your wishes on the breeze,
Let them dance with perfect ease.
In this tapestry, join the fun,
Before the setting of the sun!

Fluttering through Milky Way Meadows

Floating on a cosmic breeze,
Jokes trade places with the trees.
In meadows where stars laugh and play,
Time ticks backward, while shadows sway.

Asteroids wink with a playful cheer,
Tickling the radiance of the year.
In this galaxy of quirky sights,
Giggles spark in the moonlit nights.

Celestial critters jump and prance,
Holding hands for a silly dance.
With space dust sprinkled in their hair,
Laughter echoes everywhere!

So come along, join the jest,
In this meadow, feeling blessed.
Let your heart take a whimsical ride,
Through the universe, wide and wild!

Meadow Murmurs and Sunlit Sighs

In the field, a whisper flows,
With laughter hid in petals' prose.
Bumblebees buzz, making a scene,
While butterflies dance, all bright and keen.

A rabbit hops in a silly way,
Chasing shadows of clouds at play.
The sun winks down with golden rays,
As flowers giggle through sunny days.

A grasshopper boasts his mighty leap,
While ants march on, their secrets to keep.
The breeze weaves tales of joy, not fright,
In a meadow kissed by dazzling light.

When twilight comes, the stars they glow,
Yet still the laughter continues to flow.
As dreams float up on gentle wings,
Tomorrow waits for the joy it brings.

Ephemeral Wishes in the Air

Blowing wishes, floating free,
They tickle the nose of a nearby bee.
A child laughs with cheeks puffed wide,
As seeds take off on the soft, warm tide.

The wind carries stories, old and new,
Of socks in trees, and a runaway shoe.
Each feathered fluff, a tale untold,
In a world where the wild hearts bold.

A squirrel manages a rather large piece,
Of stolen treasure, giggling in peace.
And every tumble, a joyful jest,
In this fleeting moment, life feels blessed.

With starlight sprinkled on a giggly night,
We dream of fluffs that take to flight.
As laughter bounds in the evening air,
We weave our wishes with loving care.

Soft Serenades of the Grasslands

Underneath the warm sun's gaze,
The grass sings songs in playful sways.
A caterpillar hums a tune,
While ladybugs dance beneath the moon.

In a corner, the daisies prance,
Wearing caps in a flowery dance.
As clouds roll by, a jovial crew,
Winking at skies so fresh and blue.

A frog croaks loud its silly song,
Joining in where the giggles belong.
Each rustle and rumble a laugh so sweet,
In the grasslands, where joy and laughter meet.

As evening falls, stars pop in cheer,
While crickets chirp stories we hold dear.
In every note, a memory's born,
In the soft serenades of the morn.

Beyond the Horizon of Tomorrow

Look beyond where the wildflowers sway,
To dreams unspooled in the bright array.
With each step taken, giggles abound,
As new adventures are waiting to be found.

The clouds wear shapes of playful dreams,
A pirate ship sails on sunlit beams.
While shadows beckon with mischievous grins,
And laughter pops like bubbles in spins.

A tumbleweed rolls across the plain,
Blowing kisses in the light summer rain.
As the sun dips down with a lazy yawn,
The horizon whispers of a brand new dawn.

With voices twinkling in the evening's light,
We craft our stories till stars shine bright.
And dance to the rhythm of laughter's song,
Beyond the horizon, where we belong.

Nature's Breath of Imagination

In a field so wide and bright,
Little seeds take to flight.
They dance on whispers, up so high,
Chasing clouds across the sky.

With giggles and a playful spin,
They laugh as summer blows the wind.
Joy spills out, no need for plans,
Just frolic in the sun-kissed strands.

Swirling round like merry bees,
Floating soft with buzzing ease.
Color bursts with every sway,
Nature's jest, a grand ballet.

Oh, to tumble, twist, and glide,
What a fun and fluffy ride!
As laughter echoes wide and far,
We find joy in every spar.

Tumbleweeds of Hope

In deserts vast where tumbleweeds roll,
A hearty laugh fills every hole.
Chasing shadows, they spin and sway,
Telling tales of a lighter day.

With every bump and twist they take,
They dream of roads they'll someday make.
Scampering through the sun-baked land,
Hoping for a dance hand in hand.

A tumble here, a tumble there,
Bouncing high without a care.
Voices crackle with wild cheer,
As visions of frolics soon appear.

Their hope a breeze, so light and free,
Wandering wild, how can that be?
With laughter's pull, they travel far,
In nature's jest, they're the true stars.

Fluff and Fancy

In a kingdom of fluff where giggles bloom,
Clouds tumble down to share their room.
Fanciful puffs of joy abound,
As smiling faces gather 'round.

Each fluffball hops and jigs about,
Wiggling in with silly shout.
A waltz of whimsy in the air,
As lightness dances everywhere.

With colorful hues and playful spins,
The heart of joy lies deep within.
Each twirl a story, a laugh, a chase,
Creating smiles in this sunny place.

So toss your cares, embrace the fun,
In fluff and fancy, we are one.
Let laughter bloom, let spirits sway,
In the garden of light, we'll play all day.

A Meadow's Lullaby

In a meadow where the crickets sing,
The soft breeze whispers, a gentle fling.
Songs of joy and playful dreams,
Float on by in silver streams.

Hopping bunnies share a laugh,
In the sunlit patch, they share their craft.
With each small leap, they spring with glee,
Painting giggles for all to see.

The flowers sway, they join the tune,
Winking sweetly beneath the moon.
A lullaby of rustling leaves,
Brings smiles and warmth that never leaves.

As stars pop forth in darkened skies,
The meadow hums, a sweet surprise.
Nestled in joy, we softly sigh,
In this laughter's hug, we will fly.

Tumbles in the Golden Light

In fields where giggles dance and play,
A bouncy tumble leads the way.
The sunbeams tickle with a bright delight,
Chasing shadows, taking flight.

With hats too big that slip and slide,
We twirl around, our hearts open wide.
Grass stains on knees, we laugh and spin,
In this golden glow, there's no need to win.

Bubbles float like dreams in the air,
We jump and reach, without a care.
With every pop, a giggle breaks,
In this world of fun, only joy awakes.

Lost in the riot of silly sounds,
We leap through puddles, just goofing around.
In a land where the sun never hides,
We hold our breath for the next crazy ride.

Awakenings Beneath the Sky

Morning light peeks in, a playful tease,
Socks mismatched, how silly it leaves.
A splash of milk, too much on the floor,
We dance and slip, who could ask for more?

In a whirlwind of breakfast, toast takes flight,
A jelly smear brings laughter bright.
With freshly squeezed juice, we toast to cheer,
To morning giggles, the best time of year.

Butterflies flutter, a comical spree,
As bees buzz in circles, just like me.
We run and hide in the wild clover,
A world of wonder, forever to discover.

With a kite that's tangled, the wind in our hair,
We chase it down, without a care.
In the bluest sky, our dreams collide,
Awakening joy, like the moon and the tide.

Wistful Wishes on Soft Winds

Whispers of wishes ride the breeze,
Twirling around like mischievous leaves.
A whimsy of dreams afloat in the air,
Each puff of wind says, 'Do you dare?'

We spin and twirl beneath the sun's glare,
With silly hats, our laughter lays bare.
A dash of glitter on our noses so bright,
We tell our secrets to the stars at night.

Oh, the clocks tick slow, just for us,
Time laughs with joy, there's no need to rush.
We make a wish with each flower we find,
Chasing the giggles, leaving worries behind.

In fields of magic where stories unfold,
Every shared laugh is a treasure of gold.
We weave our tales with the softest of sighs,
In the dance of the wind, our spirits will rise.

In the Garden of Fleeting Moments

In a garden where silliness blooms with grace,
Each petal holds a laugh, a bright embrace.
The blossoms nod as we skip and prance,
We dance with daisies in a playful trance.

With watering cans that dump and splash,
We giggle together, oh what a crash!
The carrots hide, they seem so sly,
But our joyous laughter makes them shy.

Beneath the sun, we cultivate cheer,
Plucking out weeds, all our worries disappear.
In a sea of colors, we paint the day,
Whirling in joy, come what may.

As twilight whispers and shadows grow long,
We relish the laughter, the heart's true song.
In this garden of moments, fleeting but free,
We gather the giggles, just you and me.

www.ingramcontent.com/pod-product-compliance
Lightning Source LLC
Chambersburg PA
CBHW071815160426
43209CB00003B/91